THE
POCKET
NATURALIST

THE POCKET NATURALIST

First published in 2013 as *Country Wisdom*
This updated edition copyright © Summersdale Publishers Ltd, 2016

Illustrations © Shutterstock

Summersdale Publishers Ltd
46 West Street
Chichester
West Sussex
PO19 1RP
UK

www.summersdale.com

Printed and bound in the Czech Republic

ISBN: 978-1-84953-803-9

THE
POCKET
NATURALIST

FELICITY HART

summersdale

CONTENTS

INTRODUCTION

The British countryside affords some of the best landscape for walking or just getting out and about. Everywhere you look you are rewarded with breathtaking views, from sweeping valleys with their patchwork of fields, stitched together with hedges, to dense ancient woodlands alive with animals and birds. Within these pages you'll find advice on everything from how to forecast the weather by looking at cloud formations before venturing out, to tips on birdwatching and identifying flora and fauna. Each section provides an array of curious country facts and suggestions for activities and excursions to help you to get the best out of the British countryside all year round. And for those who would like to enhance their country wisdom, there is a Further Reading section which gives details of more in-depth resources.

So what are you waiting for? Have your walking boots and binoculars at the ready while you read on and let your enthusiasm take you away!

SPRING

Buttercups and daisies -
Oh, the pretty flowers,
Coming ere the spring time
To tell of sunny hours.

Mary Howitt, from 'Buttercups and Daisies'

INTRODUCTION

Spring: the marker of new beginnings, when blossoms can be seen budding on trees, and plants and flowers are breaking through the thawing earth. The first official day of spring varies each year, falling around 19–21 March, due to the earth's orientation to the sun. It's a great time to sight wildlife, such as bees, hedgehogs, frogs, toads, snakes and lizards, waking up from its winter slumber. A brand new, beautiful countryside awaits you, so put on your wellies and start exploring.

SPRING HAS SPRUNG

BLUEBELLS

A carpet of dainty bluebells is one of the most iconic and romantic images of springtime that can be enjoyed in scores of woodlands across the UK. These plants favour moist and shady conditions and, contrary to their name, can actually produce white or even pink blooms (though if they are pink, chances are the plant is the Spanish cousin of the English bluebell). The best time to see them is between late April and May, though this may vary from region to region.

COWSLIPS

You'll often see vast swathes of cowslips on motorway banks and roadside verges in April, May and June – a teaser of the yellow blankets you can find in the countryside. This pretty yellow flower likes open ground, such as fields, meadows, coastal dunes and clifftops. Its name is thought to derive from the Old English for cow dung – as the plant was often found growing among the manure in cow pastures! Closely related to the primrose, cowslips are widespread throughout Britain and Ireland, except in the far north.

COUNTRY LORE

The cowslip flower *(Primula veris)* has many reputed uses, one of the more fantastical being the ability to split rocks containing treasure.

CROCUSES

Crocus flowers are among the first to herald spring. They are easily identified by their delicate, cup-shaped blooms in shades of lilac, purple, yellow and white. There are more than 80 species of crocus and they are great at attracting bees, keeping their interiors warm by up to 10°C higher than the temperature outside to encourage nectar flow. (If you have a penchant for gardening, why not plant some of these – the bees will love you for it.)

In the country they are found in meadows and woodlands in the earlier months of spring, though some crocuses bloom in the autumn. The spice saffron is obtained from the stamens of a particular autumn-blooming crocus called *Crocus sativus* (or saffron crocus).

DAFFODILS

Daffodils are a much-loved spring flower. Another name given to them is the 'Lent lily' as their cycle often coincides with the Lenten period. Their bright yellow trumpet-shaped petals can be seen cheering up the sides of roads, and in woods and fields across Britain. While we usually associate daffodils with the colour yellow, there are about fifty species and their colours range from white and yellow to orange and even pink. These distinctive blooms are at their best in March and April.

If one daffodil is worth a thousand pleasures, then one is too few.

William Wordsworth

PRIMROSES

Primroses start flowering in earliest spring, while most other plants are just beginning to emerge from their winter slumber. They usually grow to a height of about 8–12 inches and have pale yellow flowers, though white or pink forms can sometimes be seen in nature. Primroses grow best in partial shade and damp conditions so you'll tend to find them in woodland and hedgerow settings.

SNOWDROPS

Snowdrops herald the end of winter and the beginning of spring. These tiny white flowers can often be seen poking up from beneath a layer of snow. This isn't where they get their name, however. Their proper name, *Galanthus*, comes from the Greek meaning 'milk-like flower', as the petals look like three drops of milk hanging from the stem. Snowdrops prefer cool, moist conditions and are best spotted on forest floors and along riverbanks in March and the beginning of April.

WILD CYCLAMEN

These put on a spectacular display in Mediterranean countries; Rhodes is beautifully carpeted with them in April and Athens in October. Despite the gruelling weather of the UK, this plant has become a more and more common sight over the years and is now naturalised in many areas, particularly in Kent. It has marbled leaves and upswept petals, which may be white, pink or purple. It prefers dappled shade so is often found in woodland settings. Some species of wild cyclamen, such as *Cyclamen hederifolium*, are very hardy and can survive freezing winters and last into spring.

VIOLETS

Despite its name, these flowers can range in colour from violet through to shades of blue, yellow, cream and white. They date back to 500 BC when the ancient Greeks cultivated them; now there are approximately 400–500 species of the flowering plant around the world. The most common wild violet in the UK is the dog violet. It has purple flowers and heart-shaped leaves. It flowers from April to June and it is found all over Great Britain, often in woods and hedge banks. Unlike other types of violet, the dog violet is not scented.

WILD GARLIC

Wild garlic is native to Europe and Asia and is one of the most popular wild foods in Britain. Between March and July, look out for a carpet of spear-shaped leaves and little white flowers that resemble exploding fireworks. You'll find wild garlic in damp areas, such as woodland or riverbanks. However, be careful you don't mistake it for the lily of the valley, which looks very similar but is poisonous. The main difference is that wild garlic smells of, well, garlic. If you'd like to try foraging it yourself, go to p.80 for a brief summary on safe practice and for further information there is plenty online and in other books. Always remember: if in doubt, leave it.

WILD GARLIC SOUP

Turning what you've foraged into something tasty you can eat is rewarding and fun. Why not give this recipe a go?

Ingredients

25 g butter
2 medium potatoes, cut into 1 cm cubes
1 medium onion, chopped
1 litre vegetable stock
4 big handfuls of wild garlic leaves, chopped
100 ml double cream
Salt and pepper to taste

Method

1. Heat the butter in a large saucepan until it starts to bubble. Then add the potatoes and onion and stir to coat evenly with the butter.

2. Season with salt and pepper.

3. Reduce the heat to low, cover with the lid and cook for 10 minutes until the vegetables have softened.

4. Add the stock and bring to the boil, then add the garlic and cook for 2 minutes. The leaves should appear wilted.

5. Transfer the contents from the saucepan into a bowl and mix with a hand-held blender until a consistent liquid. Then return to the pan over a low heat and stir in the cream.

6. Serve with hot, crusty bread.

WILD ORCHIDS

Orchids are among our most beautiful wild flowers. There are about 50 species in Britain and their exotic petals range in colour from pale lilac to purple. They are generally found in calcareous soils (i.e. chalk and limestone) and they flower from April to September. Orchids have a reputation for being hard to find, but you can sometimes spot them in their hundreds if the conditions are right.

WOOD ANEMONE

This pretty spring flower grows in ancient woodlands. It has a short red stem and 6–7 star-like white petals. In March and May, swathes of wood anemones can be seen on forest floors. It spreads at a rate of six feet in a hundred years – so a carpet of these wild flowers is a good indicator of ancient woodland.

People from a planet
without flowers would
think we must be mad
with joy the whole time
to have such things.

Iris Murdoch

NATURAL WEATHER INDICATORS

PINE CONES

The pine cone is one of the most reliable of all natural weather indicators. In dry weather, pine cones open out as the scales shrivel up and stand out stiffly. When it is damp, the cone returns to its normal shape.

CAN COWS PREDICT THE WEATHER?

A popular old wives' tale states that when cows sit down in a field it means that rain is on its way as they want to keep the patch of ground that they are lying on dry. They also dislike the rain on their faces, so they will sit with their backs to the rain too.

RHODODENDRONS

You can tell what temperature the air is by looking at a rhododendron plant. At 0°C the leaves are closed but as the temperature rises, the leaves unfurl. When the temperature reaches 15°C, the leaves are completely open.

FLOWER FRAGRANCE

The old saying 'Flowers smell best just before rain' has a ring of truth to it. When the air is warm and humid, a flower's scent molecules are more readily vaporised. These molecules are able to travel further when carried by a water molecule, and are easier for our noses to detect.

CLOSED PETALS

Many flowers fold their petals before it rains in order to protect their pollen. Dandelions, tulips, chickweed, wild indigo and clovers all close their blossoms before rain.

DEW

Look out for dew on the grass at sunrise. The presence of dew means it probably won't rain that day. If the grass is dry, it means clouds are around (often accompanied by rain).

It is not easy to walk alone
in the country without
musing upon something.

Charles Dickens

WHETHER THE WEATHER BE FINE

Before venturing out, look to the heavens as the clouds will provide an accurate forecast of any sudden changes in the weather, for example:

Altocumulus – a rolling mass of cloud that appears in layers or patches, which also goes by the name of 'mackerel sky' as the cloud pattern is reminiscent of the markings of a king mackerel. As the saying goes, 'Mackerel sky, mackerel sky. Never long wet and never long dry.'

Altostratus – a relatively featureless layer of middle-level, grey cloud, through which the sun, if visible, appears as if through ground glass and casts no shadows. It often thickens and becomes nimbostratus.

Cirrus – also known as 'mare's tails' as the wispy thin curly white and grey strands resemble locks of hair – a sure sign that rain is on the way.

Cumulus – these clouds are the ones that look most like they were drawn by a child: puffy, fluffy and white. They indicate fair weather – perfect for a long walk in the country.

Cumulonimbus – these clouds are often vast and dense, and will likely be mushroom-shaped. They indicate heavy rain and perhaps even thunder and lightning.

Nimbostratus – a dark grey cloud, generally at middle levels, but which may extend down towards the surface. It gives rise to prolonged periods of rain.

Stratus – a low-level layer of relatively featureless, grey cloud, which may shroud the tops of hills or even reach the ground (when it appears as fog). It may rarely give rise to drizzle or produce a fall of minute ice crystals.

COUNTRY LORE

The Old Welsh proverb *Enfys y bora, aml gawoda. Enfys y p'nawn, tegwch a gawn* translates as 'Morning rainbow may bring showers. Afternoon rainbow fine weather we'll have'.

WHAT'S AT THE END OF THE RAINBOW?

This beautiful arc of light is caused by the reflection of light in droplets of water in the atmosphere, resulting in a spectrum of coloured light. They appear during sun showers – when it rains and the sun is shining at the same time. Unfortunately it's not possible to reach the end of the rainbow because as soon as you walk towards it, it will appear to recede into the distance.

OUR FEATHERED FRIENDS

THE DAWN CHORUS

One of the loveliest signs of spring is the return of migrating birds and the dawn chorus. Have you ever wondered what the birds are saying to each other as they sing out at sunrise? It's the male songbirds that practise their falsettos, and their calls can be interpreted as either 'Keep away!' or 'Come here now!' – the latter is a serenade to any females in earshot to let them know that they have a territory of their own. The gaps in their love songs are so that they can listen for replies. The most successful males are those that can sing a loud and complex song, which shows that they are desirable mates.

BIRD AROMATHERAPY

It's not just humans who like to make their homes smell nice: female blue tits often weave aromatic plants like lavender and mint into their nests to keep them fresh and bug-free for their chicks. Starlings line their nests with the green leaves of aromatic plants such as yarrow, parsley and mint in order to keep parasites at bay. And some urban birds achieve the same effect by deliberately incorporating cigarette butts into their nests! Nicotine is a powerful natural insecticide which wards against parasites such as lice, ticks and fleas.

WONDERFUL WOODPECKERS

One of the most familiar sounds of the forest is that of the woodpecker drumming into trees for sap, insects and grubs. But did you know that the woodpecker's tongue is five times the length of its beak?

BIRDWATCHING TIPS

Invest in a good pair of lightweight binoculars – to ensure you get a pair with suitable magnification, divide the smaller number into the larger number and avoid anything less than 5, e.g. for 7x42, 42÷7 = 6. Reading up on the kinds of birds you might spot in the habitat you'll be visiting will make it easier to identify them. Take a notebook with you so that you can record what you have seen and heard; if you haven't been able to identify a sighting, draw a simple sketch or make a note of the plumage and colour so that you can work out what you saw when you get home.

COLLECTIVE NOUNS OF COMMON BIRDS

A murder of crows

A charm of finches

A confusion of guinea fowl

A party of jays

An exaltation of larks

A richness of martins

A watch of nightingales

A parliament of owls

A bouquet of pheasants

A clutter of starlings

THE WONDERS OF NATURE

SWEET AND BLOOMING

One of the prettiest trees you can encounter on a stroll in spring is the beautiful and ancient wild cherry *(Prunus avium)* – also known as the crab cherry, hawkberry or mazzard – which reveals an abundance of dainty white blossoms in early April. Its fruit, which appears later in midsummer, has been a source of sweet nutrition for humans and birds alike for centuries – indeed, part of the tree's Latin name, *'avium'*, was inspired by the close relationship that the tree enjoys with its feathered visitors.

GROWTH RINGS

As a tree grows, its trunk needs to become thicker to support the weight of its branches. It does this by adding a layer of wood, or a 'growth ring', to its trunk each year. 'Springwood' is the name given to the thin, inner layer of the ring which grows in the spring. 'Summerwood' is the name given to the darker, thicker outer layer which grows in the summer. All temperate and tropical forest trees produce growth rings in accordance with the dry seasons. Trees that grow in tropical humid rainforests do not have rings due to the fact that there is no discernible dry season, so the trees there grow continuously.

Nature never hurries.
Atom by atom, little by
little she achieves
her work.

Ralph Waldo Emerson,
from *Society and Solitude*

HOW TO DETERMINE THE AGE OF A TREE

Aside from counting the rings by removing a section of trunk, another way is to measure the circumference of the trunk approximately one and a half metres from the base. Take the measurement in centimetres and divide this number by 2.5; the result is the age of the tree. Oaks can survive for a millennium and grow upwards of 40 metres high.

NOTABLE TREES TO VISIT IN THE UK

The Ankerwycke Yew, Berkshire – at around 2,000 years old and over 30 feet wide this monster of a yew tree, which can be found in the ruins of a priory, is believed to mark the spot where King John signed the Magna Carta in 1215, as well as the place where Henry VIII conducted his trysts with Anne Boleyn.

The Mottisfont Abbey plane tree, Hampshire – this is the largest plane tree in the UK, its branches extend to over 1,500 square metres.

COUNTRY LORE

Witches are said to congregate and take shelter under elder trees, because of their magical properties. Elder wood is considered to be the most powerful conductor of magic.

POOHSTICKS

This is a simple game that can be enjoyed at any time of year and is a great way of bribing reluctant small folk to come for a country walk. Invented by A. A. Milne in the Winnie the Pooh stories and first played in the Hundred Acre Wood, it can be played on any low bridge with running water beneath. Each player drops a stick on the upstream side of the bridge, then the players rush to the downstream side, and the winner is the owner of the stick that is first to appear.

Of all the trees that
grow so fair,
Old England to adorn,
Greater is none beneath
the Sun,
Than Oak, and Ash,
and Thorn.

Rudyard Kipling, from 'A Tree Song'

NEW BEGINNINGS

Embark on a walk on an early warm spring day and you might be lucky enough to spot some animals making their first foray after hibernating over winter. Look out for frogs and toads, snakes, such as grass and adder, not to mention hedgehogs, squirrels and newly emerged queen bees.

DEER ANTLERS

Another springtime sign to look out for is shed deer antlers. There are more than two million deer living in the UK. The most common native deer is the roe deer. Male roe deer have short antlers which they shed each spring. Antlers are made of a dense bone covered with a hairy skin called 'velvet'. They are crucial to a buck or stag as he uses his antlers to fight (or rut) other males during the three-week mating season in October. As soon as the antlers are shed, a new set starts to grow immediately, reaching full size in August. Parks and woodlands are good areas to find shed antlers in March and April.

NIFTY NEWTS

Look out for newts in streams and ponds in the warmer months. There are three species of these amphibious creatures in the UK:

Great crested newt – dark brown with a warty appearance and a bright orange tummy.

Smooth newt – also brown and spotted but sports a wavy crest from its head to the tip of its tail.

Palmate newt – very similar to the smooth newt but it has a pink or yellow throat.

PROTECTED SPECIES

Newts are a protected species in the UK and it is illegal to sell or trade them in any way. Since the 1970s, newt numbers have been declining due to the large-scale loss of their breeding ponds. The great crested newt has been particularly badly affected, and it is illegal to harm or kill them, or disturb their habitat. If you intend to capture or handle a great crested newt, even if it is for survey or research purposes, you are required by law to have a licence.

HERE BE HARES

Hares are a rare sight in the British countryside as opposed to the ubiquitous rabbit. There are two species:

Brown hare – also known as the European hare, it has reddy-brown fur, dark-tipped ears and long, powerful hind legs. They are normally nocturnal, quiet creatures except in spring when  they can be seen 'boxing' each other, but it's often the females taking a swipe at the males to put them in their place. This courtship behaviour gave rise to the common phrase, 'mad as a March hare'.

Mountain hare – smaller than the brown hare but more adapted to colder, more exposed habitats, such as the Alps, the Baltics, the Highlands and Orkney. Its coat is various shades of brown but its tail remains white all year round.

COUNTRY LORE

The much-maligned common toad has been associated with supernatural powers for centuries – the 'toad stone', supposedly hidden inside the amphibian's head, is believed to change colour in the presence of poison.

MEDICINAL PLANTS

Before the advent of high-street pharmacies, country dwellers found cures for their ills in the plants that grew around them.

BIRCH

The sap of the birch tree was prized as a detoxifying tonic that cleansed the body and cleared up skin problems. The sap is still harvested today using a process called tapping, in which a hole is drilled into the trunk of the tree and the sap is collected via a tube.

DANDELION

Dandelion leaves were used in salads in order to stimulate digestion and dandelion roots were brewed into a tea or beer which was taken to relieve constipation. Dandelion juice was also a popular topical remedy for warts.

DOCK LEAVES

Dock leaves have been used to calm burns, blisters and nettle stings. The roots of the plant were also used to create a tea which was thought to cure boils.

LAVENDER

Lavender oil was used to disinfect hospitals during World War One but it is most commonly known for its relaxing properties. Lavender tea was often drunk before bedtime to aid sleep. Lavender is still a popular treatment for a wide variety of ailments today, including headaches, insect bites, insomnia and stress.

NETTLES

Nettles have been used medicinally for centuries. The leaves, seeds and roots have been used to treat a wide range of conditions including anaemia, arthritis, eczema and gout. Today, many people use it to treat urinary tract infections and hay fever, and nettle soup and nettle tea are popular health tonics.

PEPPERMINT

Chewing a few peppermint leaves was thought to relieve a toothache and peppermint tea was commonly taken for cold and flu, abdominal pain and indigestion. Peppermint oil can relax the muscles of the intestines, which is why pills containing this oil are prescribed to IBS suffers today.

That is one good thing
about this world... there
are always sure to be
more springs.

L. M. Montgomery

NOTES

....
....
....
....
....
....
....
....
....
....
....
....
....
....
....
....
....
....
....
....

....
....
....
....
....
....
....
....
....
....
....
....
....
....
....
....
....
....
....
....
....
....
....

....
....
....
....
....
....
....
....
....
....
....
....
....
....
....
....
....
....
....
....
....
....
....
....
....
....
....

SUMMER

Summer has filled her veins
with light and her heart is
washed with noon.

Cecil Day-Lewis

INTRODUCTION

Summer is a busy, bustling time of year and paired with the warmer weather it is the perfect time to spend the long days outdoors. See bees buzz from one flower to the next and butterflies roam free, discover the spiky flowers of wood sage bloom and dream of what's beyond while stargazing under the night sky. It's the time of year when nature is welcoming you to its world, so make the most of it!

HERE COMES THE SUN

SOLSTICE

One of the best but also busiest times to visit the world-famous ancient standing stones at Stonehenge in Wiltshire is during the summer solstice; the longest day of the year, when the sun rises above the Heel Stone, marking the advent of summer. 'Solstice' literally means the 'standing still' of the sun.

A PLACE OF CELEBRATION

There are many theories as to why Stonehenge was built. The most generally accepted theory is that it began some 4,000 years ago as a burial site which evolved in several construction stages over the next 1,500 years to the familiar form we see today. Stonehenge is formed of two rings: the inner ring which

comprises 3–5 ton bluestone blocks and an outer ring made up of 20–30 ton sandstone blocks. Historians are to this day perplexed by where the slabs came from and how our ancestors managed to transport them. Research suggests the bluestones come from an outcrop in Wales, whether they were transported via human labour or glaciers is still a mystery. The monument is believed to be a prehistoric temple which was deliberately built on the solstice axis in order to align with the movements of the sun.

STONEHENGE'S LITTLE SISTER

A mile away from Stonehenge, archaeologists have discovered another prehistoric site which is thought to be the 'little sister' of the famous standing stones. Researchers have dubbed this new stone circle 'Bluehenge', after the colour of the 27 Welsh stones it once incorporated. No one knows for sure why Bluehenge was built or why its 27 stones were eventually used to enlarge Stonehenge, but one hypothesis is that it was used as a massive burial site.

CHANGING THE CLOCKS

British Summer Time (BST) begins when the clocks go forward 1 hour at 1 a.m. on the last Sunday in March. This is sometimes referred to as Daylight Saving Time (DST) as there is more daylight in the evenings and less in the mornings. The clocks go back 1 hour at 2 a.m. on the last Sunday in October. When the clocks go back, the UK is on Greenwich Mean Time (GMT).

WHAT A TIME SAVER!

British builder William Willett pioneered the introduction of DST in 1905. He published a pamphlet in 1907 entitled 'A Waste of Time' in which he advised the reader to make the most of summer by getting up earlier. It's thought that Willett's passionate plea for an extra hour of  sunlight was partly fuelled by the fact that he was a keen golfer and he was fed up of having his games cut short in the winter! The British did eventually embrace Willet's idea in 1916, after Germany and Austria-Hungary implemented Daylight Savings Time as a way to conserve coal during wartime. Daylight Saving Time is now in use in over 70 countries worldwide and over 1 billion people have to deal with the twice-yearly shift.

If you struggle to remember which direction to change your clock, there's a trick which can help. Simply memorise the phrase, 'Spring forward, fall back'.

To sit in the shade on a fine day and look upon the verdant green hills is the most perfect refreshment.

Jane Austen

A STORM IS BREWING

THUNDER AND LIGHTNING

Be mindful of stormy weather conditions when you embark on a long walk in summer; although the chances of being struck by lightning are very low, it's always worth knowing what you can do to avoid it:

- If there are any solid structures nearby – such as a church – seek shelter and wait half an hour after the last rumble of thunder before venturing out again.

- If there is no cover and you are in woodland, avoid sheltering under tall or isolated trees and look for some lower-level trees instead.

- Steer clear of open spaces, such as fields, and stay away from water and any metal objects, such as fencing.

FLOWERS IN ABUNDANCE

SWEET REMEDY

Summer is the season of hay fever, but one way to combat this that some sufferers swear by is to eat a daily spoonful of locally produced honey. The idea is that the honey behaves like a vaccine – pollen spores from the multiple flowers that grow in the area find their way into the honey, which when eaten helps build up immunity to local allergens that trigger hay fever. So, if the thought of walking in the countryside in the summer is enough to make your eyes run, invest in some local honey and test the theory.

SUMMER BLOOMS

Aside from the exotic orchids, there are some spectacular floral displays in the summer, most notably:

Buttercup – very common yellow flower with five waxy petals.

Campion – dark pink flowers with five deeply notched petals.

Foxglove – tall spikes with multiple pink tubular flowers, with dark speckles inside the tubes.

Clover – spiky ball-shaped flowers, which can be white, purple, red or yellow.

Ox-eye daisy – large version of the traditional daisy.

Corn marigold – flower head is not dissimilar to the daisy except it's mainly yellow with white-tipped petals.

Feverfew – very reminiscent of the daisy but with rounder petals and citrus-scented leaves.

FOXGLOVES

The foxglove is a common plant, found in the garden and in the wild. Its generic name is *Digitalis*, which comes from the Latin for finger *(digitus)*, a reference to the thimble-shaped flowers which look as if you could slip your finger right inside.

Foxgloves are highly poisonous to humans and animals. However, an extract from the plant is used in the drug digoxin, which is prescribed for heart failure patients. This drug has to be administered under the strictest of conditions as the medicinal dose that is required is very close to the lethal dose.

Death by digitalin (the poison found in common foxglove) is one of Agatha Christie's favourite murder methods. In her novel *Postern of Fate*, a character is poisoned when foxglove leaves are mixed into her salad. In *The Herb of Death*, foxglove leaves are mixed with sage leaves and used to stuff a roast duck for a dinner party.

COUNTRY LORE

The origins of the name 'foxglove' is surrounded by mythology. Some claim that naughty fairies gave a fox the flower petals to put onto his toes so that he could sneak into the chicken house without being heard.

THOSE DELICATE WINGED INSECTS

BEAUTIFUL BUTTERFLIES

Look out for butterflies in the summer months; there are around 59 species in the UK. Grow clumps of brightly coloured plants and shrubs to attract them into your garden, most notably buddleia, milkweed, black-eyed Susan, lavender and Dutchman's pipe, and create an area for them to sun themselves – a sunny patio sheltered from the wind is ideal.

SPOTTING BUTTERFLIES

The most common butterfly in British gardens is the small white *(Pieris rapae)*, closely followed by the large white *(Pieris brassicae)*, both commonly known as the cabbage white butterfly. Other butterflies which are frequently seen include the gatekeeper, meadow brown, common blue, peacock, green-veined white, red admiral, small tortoiseshell and the ringlet.

Small white – the bane of allotment holders everywhere. The larvae of this creamy white butterfly have a voracious appetite and will bore into cabbage, kale, radish, broccoli and horseradish. It is widespread throughout Britain, except the far north.

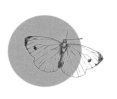

Large white – a strong flier and can be seen throughout Great Britain. It can be distinguished from the small white by its larger size and the larger black tip on its forewing.

Gatekeeper – orange and brown with a black eyespot on its forewing, this butterfly is also known as the hedge brown. It spends much of its time in the summer months basking with its wings open. It can be found wherever shrubs grow close to rough grassland.

Meadow brown – the meadow brown is one of our most common and widespread butterflies. It is orange and brown, with a black eyespot on forewing tip. It can be distinguished from the hedge brown by the single white pupil in its eyespot.

Common blue – as its name suggests, this butterfly is the most common blue found in Britain. Males are an iridescent blue, whereas females are primarily brown with variable amounts of 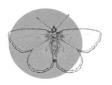 blue. This species is found in grassland habitats, such as meadows, woodland clearings and sand dunes.

 **Peacock** – red-winged peacock butterflies are one of our most recognisable species due to the spectacular eyespots on their fore and hindwings. It's thought that the eyespots evolved to scare off predators. This beautiful butterfly is a familiar sight in gardens across Britain.

Green-veined white – this butterfly is often mistaken for its cousin, the small white. It can be found in parks and gardens from spring through to autumn. The green veins of colour on the underside of its wings, which distinguishes it from  the small white, are actually composed of yellow and black scales.

Red admiral – with its velvety black wings intersected with red bands, this striking butterfly is easy to spot. Red admirals are frequently seen in gardens throughout the British Isles but it can be found almost anywhere – from coastal regions to the tops of mountains.

Small tortoiseshell – a well-known butterfly in Britain and Ireland. It has bright orange and black patterned wings with a small white patch on its forewings. It is one of the first butterflies to be seen in spring.

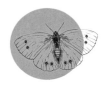

Ringlet – the 'rings' on this chocolate brown butterfly give its common name. Its underwings have distinctive eyespots which have a white centre, black inner ring and yellow outer ring. Its dark colouration means it warms up quickly, which is why it is one of the few butterflies to fly on overcast days. It is typically found in sheltered and damp spots.

Nature always wears the colours of the spirit.

Ralph Waldo Emerson, from *Nature*

DOWN ON THE FARM

CROPS

When out walking, it's important to respect that a farmer's crops are his livelihood, so always walk round the edge of the field, however tempting it is to run across an expanse of ripe barley! Barley has a high commercial value – not only is it used as a staple feed grain for livestock, it can also be 'malted' for use in various breads, beers and whiskies.

COWS

There are a number of breeds of cow that can be seen in the patchwork of farmland that makes up much of the UK. Here are the most common breeds:

Charolais – this stocky French breed has a white coat and endearing pointy-out ears.

Hereford – a breed which dates from Roman times. It has a rich red-brown coat and a white face.

Friesian – this black-and-white dairy cow became prevalent in the UK after being introduced in the nineteenth century from northern Holland.

Highland – this hardy Scottish breed has an impressive set of horns and a long wiry coat to cope with cold temperatures.

Jersey – A fawn-coloured dairy cow originally from Jersey in the Channel Islands.

DO BULLS SEE RED?

If you see a bull while wearing a red jacket, don't be scared: bulls are actually colour-blind. They're attracted to movement, rather than colour, so if a bull charges at you it is a good idea to throw something like a jacket away from yourself. The bull should be distracted by the movement and chase the object instead.

AVOIDING MOODY MOOS

Cows have had a bad press in recent years, with stories of walkers being threatened or even trampled by them. Cows can be very aggressive, particularly if a mother is separated from its calf. If you have a dog with you, keep it on a tight leash. Rather than walking through the middle of the field, walk round the edge and at a slow pace so as not to frighten the herd.

UNUSUAL FARM ANIMALS IN THE BRITISH COUNTRYSIDE

If you're lucky, you might see one or more of the following when walking near a farm:

Alpaca – this docile creature from South America is often placed in fields with sheep as their towering presence scares away foxes.

Ostrich – encountering a field of these prehistoric-looking birds can be quite menacing, but they are farmed for their meat and eggs throughout the UK.

Water buffalo – this impressive handlebar-horned creature is particularly docile, making it ideal for milking.

NATURE'S NASTIES

SNAKES ON A PLAIN!

There are three species of snake native to the UK. They mostly feed on small mammals and birds and can be found across different terrains – grassland, woods and near water.

Adder – the only poisonous snake living wild in the UK. To be bitten by this diamond-marked creature is incredibly rare but it is likely that the unlucky recipient would require hospital treatment.

Grass snake – a good swimmer and feeds almost exclusively on amphibians, playing dead when it feels threatened.

Smooth snake – this spotted snake constricts its prey to death.

One thing is certain about going outdoors. When you come back in, you'll be scratching.

P. J. O'Rourke, from 'The Outdoors and How It Got There'

BUG BITES

Summer is when insects are out in force, making it the season for bites and stings. Here are a few tips on how to reduce your chances of being nibbled or stung:

Avoid wearing bright, rough-textured clothing, as insects are attracted to these – wear pale colours and smooth or silky fabrics instead.

Eat garlic or onions – this will alter the smell of your sweat, giving it a distinctly savoury smell, which will repel sweet-loving insects.

STINGERS!

Nettle stings are more likely to occur while out walking in the summer, when you're sporting shorts and T-shirts. The leaves are covered in silky hollow hairs containing chemicals which cause a burning, itching feeling on the skin when brushed against. Dock leaves always grow near to nettles and the leaves, when rubbed on the affected area, have a cooling effect. If the irritation persists, the pulp from an aloe vera plant is also very effective, if you have the plant at home.

A CAMPING ADVENTURE

Summer is the ideal season to go camping – the days are long and the nights are (hopefully) warm. However, your camping expedition can easily be ruined by a few rookie mistakes when pitching your tent. Here are a few tips to ensure the best night's sleep possible:

PRACTICE RUN

Putting up a tent can be a challenge at the best of times let alone when it's blowing a gale! Try assembling it in your garden or local park before you head into the great outdoors. This will also give you the chance to check you have all the gear you need (tip: make a list of all the items you need to take with you and check these items off as you pack your car). Most tent poles are now colour coded so that it's easy to know which pole slots into which sleeve. If yours aren't colour coded, consider some DIY colour coding to help you pitch your tent in record time.

PITCH PERFECT

Once you arrive at your site, don't pitch yourself too close to the washing facilities and toilet blocks – unless you fancy being woken by  people walking to and fro late at night and early in the morning. Don't pitch your tent as far away as possible either – this is where large groups and/or people who plan to stay up late and party are likely to head. Aim for a position which is somewhere in between.

FLAT GROUND

Once you've chosen your spot, lie down on the ground to check there are no lumps and bumps. You ideally want level, slightly soft  ground with no rocks or hidden holes. If you have to set up home on a slope, sleep with your head uphill and your feet downhill. This will be the most comfortable position to sleep in and it will stop you from sliding down the hill sideways during the night and waking up wedged into one side of the tent!

WIND BREAK

The noise of flapping fabric can keep you awake all night. Position your tent so that the entrance doesn't face into the wind. Use a hedge as a wind break if necessary. When pegging out the tent, tap the pegs in diagonally at a 45 degree angle, pointing downwards towards the tent. Peg out the back corners first and then work your way forwards. Peg out the guy lines which hang from the side of the tent last of all. These will give you added stability in high winds. You can mark them with reflective tape if you worried about tripping over them in the dark.

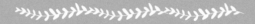

People must feel
that the natural world
is important and
valuable and beautiful
and wonderful and
an amazement and
a pleasure.

David Attenborough

GO BATTY

There are many organised bat walks around the country in the summer months. Dusk and dawn are peak times for bat sightings as the nocturnal insects that they feed on are most active then. Bats like to fly in circular formation while feeding – listen out for their distinctive fluttering sound. Look out for bats roosting in tree hollows and hedgerows as well as derelict buildings.

Bats are very common in the tropics: there are 225 species of bats in Indonesia, Venezuela has 145 and Mexico is home to 140 species. There are seventeen native bat species in the UK; the most common species are the common pipistrelle and the brown long-eared bat. For more information on organised bat walks and where to spot bats, visit www.bats.org.uk.

Alcathoe bat – very similar to the whiskered and Brandt's bat species, it has slightly shaggy fur

Barbastelle – this bat is known for its pug-like features and large wide ears.

Bechstein's bat – usually only found in parts of southern England and south-east Wales, this bat is one of the rarest in the UK.

Brandt's bat – only separated as distinct species from the whiskered bat in 1970.

Brown long-eared bat – it lives up to its namesake and has exceptionally good hearing. It has been said that this bat can hear a ladybird walking on a leaf!

Common pipistrelle bat – these bats are very common in Britain and can be spotted by their fast and jerky flight.

Daubenton's bat – also known as the water bat, as it fishes for insects with its large feet and tail.

Greater horseshoe bat – one of the largest bats in the UK, it can be distinguished by its size and horseshoe-shaped nose leaf.

Grey long-eared bat – as its name suggest, this little bat is grey and has sizeable ears. It also has a dark face.

Leisler's bat – also known as the 'hairy armed bat', due to the fur that covers its limbs. It also has mane-like fur around its head and neck.

Lesser horseshoe bat – unlike its big cousin, the greater horseshoe, this bat can often been seen with its face fully covered by its wings.

Nathusius' pipistrelle – a migratory species that resembles the common pipistrelle but is slightly larger in size.

Natterer's bat – it has broad wings that enables it to fly much slower than other bats, helping to hunt prey more efficiently. It even snacks on spiders!

Noctule bat – this bat has long narrow wings that enable it to fly with precision and speed. It's the largest bat in the UK.

Serotine bat – this laid-back bat has a distinctive flapping flight and is one of the largest species in the UK.

Soprano pipistrelle bat – the difference between this and the common pipistrelle is mostly down to its higher-frequency echolocation call.

Whiskered bat – contrary to its name, the whiskered bat does not have long, cat-like whiskers! It is rarely seen in the UK, but when spotted it may be hard to distinguish from the Brandt's bat.

BATS OF THE WORLD

Although bats are a commonly misunderstood creature, in China they are a symbol of good fortune. They aren't listed as a protected species in many countries and numbers are falling increasingly due to extreme weather conditions and the loss of its natural habitat.

Egyptian fruit bat – found in Africa, India and Pakistan, this bat is relatively small (around six inches) but its wings span two feet. They are often nicknamed the flying fox due to their vulpine features.

Tent-making bats – these bats can be spotted in Central and South America. They are so-called because they build 'tents' or roosts out of leaves by weakening both sides of the stem with their teeth and pulling the halves down over them.

Vampire bats – the main thing to know about these bats is that they don't live in Transylvania; in fact, they live in Central and South America. They do feed on blood, but hardly ever human's blood – instead they prefer that of cattle, horses, pigs and birds.

COUNTRY LORE

In European folklore bats have long been associated with witchcraft and described as witches' familiars, but in Chinese culture they are regarded as symbols of luck and prosperity. An old wives' tale suggest that bats will fly at people, given the opportunity, so that they can entangle themselves in human hair!

Those who contemplate the beauty of the Earth find reserves of strength that will endure as long as life lasts.

Rachel Carson, from *Lost Woods*

WATERSIDE WILDLIFE

Rivers, ponds and lakes are teeming with life in summer. Take an afternoon stroll along a river to see barbel leaping to catch flies or look out for carp cruising near to the surface of a pool. If you're quiet you may spot a spritely water vole at the water's edge or quietly paddling, and keep an eye and an ear out for the majestic kingfisher perched on a branch or darting into the water to catch the small fry that are abundant at this time of year.

TRACKS AND SIGNS

If you know what you're looking for, there are signs of wildlife everywhere. The soft mud near rivers is perfect for spotting animal tracks – here are some tips of things to look out for next time you go for a stroll:

- A paw print with five toes could be an otter or a badger. If there is a large pad behind the toe pads, it's probably a badger.

- A paw print with four toes could belong to a fox or a dog. Look at the size of the rear pad – foxes have rear pads which are the same size as their toe pads, where as a dog's rear pad is larger.

- Deer tracks are easily identifiable by the two sausage-shaped slots made by their hooves.

Aside from tracks, look out for burrows near the water's edge, often with a patch of nibbled grass around the entrance, and piles of grass and stems with diagonal cuts at the end. These are all signs of water voles. Rats dig similar holes to water voles but they often have a heap of soil outside the entrance and the holes are connected by well-trampled paths. It is rare to see an otter but you might see their droppings (or spraints). These are 2–7 cm long and contain fish bone and scales. They smell very strongly of fish!

It is pleasant to have
been to a place the way
a river went.

Henry David Thoreau

SCRUMMY SUMMER FOOD

SUMMER SALAD

There are many wild flowers and herbs that can be picked and eaten safely the year round. If you're curious about foraging for food in the great outdoors, it's advisable to do some research, or even attend a course, before getting down to the eating. However, there are many safe, easy pickings to be had in summer: wild garlic bulbs (see p.18 for a tasty wild garlic soup recipe) can be harvested, elderflowers can be eaten raw or made into a plethora of sweet-tasting condiments and the dainty, pink mallow flower can brighten and bulk up any salad dish.

FORAGING BASICS

If you fancy having a go at foraging your own food, here are a few tips to ensure your experience is a safe and happy one:

- **The four fs** – by law you are able to forage for the four fs, which are fruit, flowers, foliage and fungi. You can forage anywhere, providing you have the right to be on the land or have permission from the landowner.

- **Don't eat what you don't know** – only eat a plant or berry if you are 100 per cent sure what it is. Some plants are toxic and can make you very ill. Consult a comprehensive guidebook or qualified guide to ensure you know what you are eating.

- **Medication** – if you are taking any medicines, be aware that some wild plants may affect the efficacy of your medication or stop its therapeutic effect altogether. It's always better to err on the safe side. If in doubt, leave it out.

- **Allergies** – some people are allergic to certain wild foods. If you are trying something for the first time, make sure you have someone with you so that they can get help should you have an adverse reaction. It's always a good idea to reserve a little of the food so that you can show the doctor what you have ingested.

- **Children** – children generally have less of a tolerance to wild plants than adults. For this reason, small children should only eat a palm-sized portion.

- **How much to gather** – it's tempting to pick a basketful of wild food when you're faced with an abundance of plants, berries or leaves. However, many wild plants need only to be picked in small quantities to be used as a flavour or a garnish. As you gain experience, and learn how much you need to pick or use in a dish, your confidence in this area will grow.

- **Safety** – it's essential that you collect your wild food from safe areas. Avoid busy roadsides as, apart from the obvious danger of being hit by a car, the plant may be tainted with exhaust fumes. Be similarly cautious of collecting anything that is growing on edge of a farmer's field due to the pesticides that are used. And obviously, steer clear of picking plants in areas where a dog may have been walked, unless the plants are high up off the ground!

HOMEMADE ELDERFLOWER CORDIAL

This cordial is delicious diluted with still or sparkling water. It can also be used as a flavouring in desserts such as ice creams and fruit fools.

Ingredients

2.5 kg white sugar, either granulated or caster
2 unwaxed lemons
20 fresh elderflower heads
85 g citric acid (available from chemists)

Method

1. Place the sugar and 1.5 litres of water into a large saucepan. Heat gently, stirring every now and again, until the sugar has dissolved. Don't let the water boil. While you are heating the water-sugar mixture, zest the lemons and then slice them into rounds. Once the sugar has dissolved, bring the pan to the boil and then turn off the heat.

2. Gently swish the elderflower heads in cold water to remove any dirt or bugs. Remove the flowers, shake off any excess water, and place the flowers in the sugar syrup, along with the lemons, zest and citric acid. Stir well, then cover and leave to infuse for 24 hours.

3. Strain the syrup through a clean tea towel or fine muslin cloth into a bowl. Fill some sterilised bottles with the drained syrup, using a funnel. (Sterilise bottles by running them through the dishwasher or washing them in boiling hot, soapy water. Rinse, then leave to dry in a low oven.)

4. Drink the cordial straight away (once opened, it will keep in a fridge for up to 6 weeks) or store your sealed bottles in a cool, dark place for a few weeks. To make your cordial keep for longer, freeze the cordial in plastic containers or ice cube trays and defrost as needed.

Look deep into nature, and then you will understand everything better.

Albert Einstein

NOTES

....

....

....

....

....

....

....

....

....

....

....

....

....

....

....

....

....

....

....

....

....

....

....

....

....
....
....
....
....
....
....
....
....
....
....
....
....
....
....
....
....
....
....
....
....
....
....
....

AUTUMN

Delicious autumn! My very
soul is wedded to it, and
if I were a bird I would fly
about the earth seeking the
successive autumns.

George Eliot

INTRODUCTION

This season can always promise beautiful sights, and the countryside offers plenty as the leaves burst into a colourful display of reds, oranges and yellows. Although the temperature is falling, you'll still see deer, boar and bats seeking a mate while hedgehogs and dormice can be spotted searching for fruit and nuts respectively to prepare for the cold months to come. Don your wellies, don't forget your anorak and have fun crunching your way through autumn.

SPECTACULAR TREES

Trees are the most notable living objects in the countryside. They are an important part of the ecosystem, providing essential habitats and food for many organisms. They also stabilise the soil and play an important part in climate control. Trees have been in existence for 370 million years and it is estimated that there are 3 trillion mature trees in the world. Since the start of human agriculture 12,000 years ago, the number of trees worldwide has decreased by 46 per cent.

Most botanists define a tree as a perennial plant (i.e. a plant that lives for more than two years) with an elongated stem, or woody trunk, which supports branches and leaves at some distance from the ground. The world's tallest known living tree is a redwood in Northern California which stands at 115.61 m (379.3 ft) high. It is estimated to be roughly 700–800 years old. Most trees are long-lived and many trees are several thousand years old. The oldest known tree in the world is a bristlecone pine in California's White Mountains, which is thought to be almost 5,000 years old. For its protection, its exact location is a secret!

HOW TO IDENTIFY A TREE BY ITS LEAVES

Trees can be split into two main groups – coniferous and broadleaved. Broadleaves, such as oak and beech, tend to produce flowers and fruit (acorns and berries) whereas most conifers produce their seeds inside cones. The easiest way to tell the two groups apart is by the shape of their leaves. The leaves of conifers are generally long and narrow, like needles, whereas the leaves of broadleaves are broad and flat (hence the name). In addition, most broadleaves tend to lose their leaves in the autumn, whereas conifers retain their needles, replacing them slowly throughout the year. There are exceptions to these rules. For example, gorse is a broadleaf tree which has needle-shaped leaves, and holly is a broadleaf which keeps its leaves all year round.

Conifers are distinctive looking as they are ideally adapted to freezing temperatures. The conical shape of the tree ensures that snow falls off the branches rather than settling heavily and damaging branches. Coniferous trees also have resins in their sap which act as a kind of antifreeze, preventing ice crystals from forming inside the cells and causing internal damage.

Leaves are verbs that conjugate the seasons.

Gretel Ehrlich, from
The Solace of Open Spaces

WHY DO BROADLEAF LEAVES CHANGE COLOUR AND DROP?

The green colour of leaves in spring and summer comes from chlorophyll, a pigment which allows a plant to produce food (glucose) through photosynthesis. As autumn draws near and there's less sunlight, chlorophyll is no longer produced and other colours that were there all along start to come through.

Broadleaf trees drop their leaves in the autumn in order to avoid damage to the fragile leaf cells due to internal ice formation. A layer forms at the base of the leaf stem, called the separation layer, and severs the tissue that connects the leaf to the branch. When the leaf falls off a scar seals the area and protects the tree from moisture loss.

AUTUMN COLOURS

The spectacular hue of autumn leaves is due to various pigments: carotenoid (orange-yellow colours) and anthocyanin (red-purple colours). Many areas around the world are famed for their vibrant autumn foliage. In Eastern Canada and the New England region of the United States, the fall colours are at their peak in October and tourists (often referred to as 'leaf peepers') flock to the area. In Japan, the ancient capital of Kyoto is awash with sensational red, gold and yellow leaves which are just as stunning as the cherry blossom in spring.

In Britain, some of the best places to see spectacular colours are arboretums, national parks and gardens, and ancient forests such as the Forest of Dean in Gloucestershire and the New Forest in Hampshire. The vibrancy of the display each year is due to a combination of factors, including soil type, sunlight, moisture and wind conditions. Head to any area that has a mix of ash, oak, sweet chestnut, beech and hawthorn and you should be rewarded with a riot of leafy splendour from mid-October onwards.

ANIMAL ANTICS

SECRETIVE SQUIRRELS

Squirrels are known for being great hoarders of seeds and nuts, but they can also be a little forgetful as to where they have hidden their treasure. As a happy consequence, millions of trees are planted by these furry tree-dwellers accidentally each year! A squirrel is very guarded about its nuts and it will even make elaborate displays of burying non-existent nuts and seeds to throw its rivals off the scent.

RED OR GREY OR BLACK?

Grey squirrels are the dominant species of squirrel in the UK with a population of over two and a half million, compared with around 150,000 of the smaller red squirrels. It is thought that the larger grey squirrels took over the food resources relied upon by the reds, and nowadays it is rare to see a red squirrel in England. They can still be seen in parts of Scotland and on the Isle of Wight.

Red squirrels are also found throughout much of Europe. However, these populations are already under threat as the grey squirrel spreads to northern Italy,

France, Switzerland and Germany. This is a serious concern. Aside from muscling out their smaller cousins, grey squirrels feed on bird eggs and chicks and cause irreparable damage to broadleaved trees such as oak, beech and sweet chestnut by stripping the tree bark.

The black squirrel, which is the same size and has the same temperament as the grey squirrel, is a relatively new type of squirrel to call Britain home. It was introduced into the UK in the early twentieth century from North America. Despite its recent introduction, the black squirrel population is soaring and grey squirrels could soon be getting a taste of their own medicine as experts predict the black squirrel could eventually become the dominant variety.

DEER

Though there are six species of deer that have established themselves in the UK, only two – roe deer and red deer – are truly native. Roe deer, with their red summer coats and yellow-spotted, dull grey winter coats, were once almost extinct in the British Isles. They can now be found in many woodlands, forests and even fields across the country. The much larger red deer (which are in fact the largest of all the land mammals in Britain) are quite similar in colour to the roe, but easily distinguished, especially the stag which grows impressive, high-branched antlers. They are most frequently spotted in the Scottish Highlands, the Lake District and East Anglia.

CLASHING OF HORNS

Autumn is rutting season for deer. This violent display occurs when stags lock horns in their annual fight for supremacy and dominance over of the largest harem of female deer. Often taking place in the early morning and the evening, there are many places to view this impressive spectacle. In the UK, deer parks owned by the National Trust and Royal Society for the Protection of Birds (RSPB) reserves make spotting this event more accessible. The chance of happening upon this magnificent display in the wild is much smaller, but that makes it all the more special! Make sure you keep at a good distance from the rutting and be aware that male deer are generally very aggressive at this time of year.

SPOTTING DEER

Deer are not always easy to see but there are signs of their presence that you can look out for, such as a horizontal 'browse line' on trees and shrubs where the deer have been feeding on buds and leaves. (Bear in mind

that deer sometime stand on their hind legs to feed, so the line might be higher up than you'd imagine.) Deer also use regular paths, called 'racks', which can often be seen at woodland boundaries, or as tunnels in dense undergrowth. Keep your eyes peeled for droppings. These black, shiny pellets are often left in small piles on tracks in woods. They are usually quite small and cylindrical and are sometimes pointed at one end and indented at the other.

COUNTRY LORE

The Celts revered deer, calling them 'fairy cattle', and some Christians view the deer as a symbol of Christ.

MIGRATION NATION

Autumn is an exciting time in the wildlife calendar as tens of millions of birds arrive in Britain. Some travel thousands of miles from Scandinavia, the Arctic and northern Europe to stay for winter, and others (referred to as 'passage visitors') stop for a few weeks to refuel before heading off to continue their journey.

MURMURING OF WINGS

Starlings flock together throughout the winter months for protection and warmth. This turns into an awesome spectacle – known as a 'murmuration' – when thousands of birds wheel through the skies, creating vast swathes of black at dawn and dusk. Other common birds flock and roost together in the winter months, such as tits, pied wagtails and wrens, but not in such impressive numbers.

I go to nature to be
soothed and healed,
and to have my
senses put in order.

John Burroughs, from *The Gospel of Nature*

SPOTTER'S GUIDE

Bewick's swan
Migrates from: Northern Siberia
Migration distance to UK: 4,023 km
Bewick's swans begin arriving in October. They are the smallest swans to visit the UK and they can usually be spotted in wet areas and farmland. The adults are white all over and the young are greyish with a pink bill. They head back to their breeding grounds in Siberia in the spring.

Brent goose
Migrates from: Canadian Arctic
Migration distance to UK: 3,000 km
Brent geese arrive in October to winter here before returning to the Canadian Arctic in April. They have dark bodies and a black head, with either a pale or dark belly. They are mainly found on the coasts of northern, eastern and southern England and in Northern Ireland.

Fieldfare

Migrates from: Scandinavia and occasionally northwest Russia
Migration distance to UK: Over 1,800 km

Hundreds of thousands of fieldfares begin to arrive from October onwards to take advantage of our warmer climate. These impressive birds are members of the thrush family. They have a grey head and neck, brown wings, a black tail and a heavily speckled front. They can be seen throughout the UK, often feeding on hawthorn berries, before returning to their breeding grounds in Scandinavia in March.

Curlew sandpiper

On passage from: Arctic Siberia
On passage to: Africa

The curlew sandpiper is a 'passage bird' or 'passage visitor'. It breeds on the tundra of Arctic Siberia and can be seen mainly along the east coast of England in August and September, before continuing on to Africa for the winter. These small waders are usually found in salt marshes and shallow coastal lagoons. The adults have a pale grey body with a white belly and a long, down-curved bill.

Black tern
On passage from: Europe and Asia
On passage to: Africa
This small tern has a black head
and silver-grey wings, back and tail.
It feeds by dipping to the water to pluck insects and small fish from the surface. Black terns can be seen near freshwater lakes and reservoirs from mid-summer to early autumn before leaving to winter in Africa.

SPOTTING TROUT

There are several different types of trout in the UK and they have different patterns and colours which change according to their environment.

Brown trout – this freshwater fish is indigenous to Europe but has been introduced to suitable locations across the world. It is a streamlined, yellow-brown fish with lots of black, orange or red spots and a pale belly. Sea trout are the same species but migrate to the sea for most of their lives, coming back to freshwater to spawn.

Ferox trout – this trout lives up to its name, which literally means 'ferocious'. It is very rare and is an evolved species of the brown trout, which it often feeds on.

Rainbow trout – this is native to North America but, like the brown trout, it can be spotted in many global freshwater areas. They are generally blue-green or yellow-green and can be identified by the pink streak along their sides.

Brook trout – this distinctive-looking fish, with a marbled pattern a long its back, bright red dappling along its flanks and a red belly is also native to North America.

Tiger trout – a hybrid of the brown trout and the brook trout, although its markings are very unique and resemble a tiger's print. Interestingly tiger trout cannot reproduce with each other.

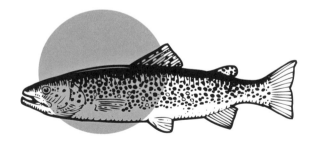

FORAGING

COMPLETELY CONKERS

Autumn is the season when the mahogany-coloured fruits of the horse chestnut tree *(Aesculus hippocastanum)* are gathered up for doing battle in the playground (at least for those schools that allow it!). A conker is usually prepared by boring a hole through the centre before threading it on a length of string. Myths abound on how to supercharge your conker, from pickling it in vinegar to baking it in the oven for half an hour, but that's not very sporting! Horse chestnuts are poisonous and not to be confused with the sweet chestnut. You can tell the difference by their husks: conkers are cased in a warty shell with short spikes, while chestnuts have spiny shells.

SWEET CHESTNUTS

Sweet chestnuts are ripe for picking and eating between September and November. They can be eaten raw, but this is an acquired taste as they are quite woody. Before preparing the chestnuts for eating, you first need to remove the burrs (the spiky casing) using a sharp knife. To cook the nuts, slice an X into the shell – this is important as the nut will explode otherwise. Place the chestnuts on a baking tray and put in a preheated oven at 200°C for around half an hour. Once cooked, the skin should peel away easily. They're best eaten warm.

BERRY GOOD

Blackberries and mulberries are the most common of the 'wild' fruits to be found on a country walk. These fruiting hedgerow plants are heavy with berries in late summer/early autumn, which can be made into crumbles, jellies to accompany meat and jams for puddings. Elderberries are also ripe for harvesting. These  bitter berries, which are purple in colour, can be used in wine-making and for making a sour jelly.

HEDGEROW JAM

This fruity jelly can be used in a variety of ways – spread it on toast, dollop it on rice pudding, stir it into porridge, or try it with cold meats and pâté.

Ingredients

A variety of picked fruit (e.g. blackberries, sloes, elderberries, damsons, rosehips)

An equal weight of cooking apples or crab apples
Granulated sugar

You will also need a jelly bag or muslin

Method

1. Wash the hedgerow fruit, and wash and slice the apples (no need to peel or core).

2. Place all the fruit in a preserving pan with a little water and simmer until the fruit is soft and has released its juices.

3. Pour into a jelly bag or muslin and strain overnight – avoid the temptation to squeeze the jelly bag as this makes the jam cloudy.

4. Measure the juice and return to the pan.

5. Add 500 g of sugar per 600 ml of juice and dissolve the sugar in the juice over a low heat.

6. Once the sugar has dissolved, boil rapidly until setting point is reached. To test the setting point, push the jelly with your fingertip: if it has formed a layer that wrinkles with pressure then you know it's done.

7. Pour into sterilised jars (see p.83 for how to sterilise jars) and seal. Use within 12 months and refrigerate after opening.

I trust in nature for the
stable laws of beauty and
utility. Spring shall plant
and autumn garner to the
end of time.

Robert Browning

FEASTING ON FUNGI

Wild mushrooms don't just look pretty, they can also be delicious! Before even considering harvesting any wild mushrooms, ensure that you get hold of a properly illustrated identification guide. When harvesting different mushrooms at once, always group them by type, and once you're sure they are edible and are ready for cooking, retain a raw specimen for reference. In the UK, some delicious varieties of edible wild mushrooms include chanterelle, shaggy inkcap, puffball and penny bun.

ROSE HIPS

Rose hips are the bright red fruit of the rose plant. They can be used to make jams, jellies and, being rich in antioxidants and vitamin C, they make an excellent ingredient for herbal tea. The hairs inside the hip are used to make itching powder!

Rose Hip Syrup

This fruity, floral syrup is great trickled over porridge or pancakes for breakfast. Use it to sweeten plain yoghurt or drizzle it over rice pudding or vanilla ice cream for a moreish dessert.

Ingredients

1 kg rose hips, washed and chopped
1 kg caster sugar

You will also need two jelly bags or muslin

Method

1. Place the chopped rose hips in a large saucepan and add 1.25 litres of water. Bring to the boil, then simmer for 15 minutes.

2. Strain through a jelly bag or a layer of folded muslin (be patient: this may take a good half an hour).

3. Pass the strained juice through another jelly bag or double layer of muslin.

4. Measure the rose hip juice and place in a large saucepan.

5. For every 500 ml of juice, add 325 g sugar.

6. Heat slowly, stirring.

7. Once the sugar has dissolved, bring to the boil and boil hard for 3 minutes.

8. Pour into warmed, sterilised bottles or jars and seal (see p.83 on how to sterilise).

9. Use within 4 months and refrigerate once opened.

Nor rural sights alone, but
rural sounds,
Exhilarate the spirit,
and restore
The tone of languid nature.

William Cowper

NOTES

....
....
....
....
....
....
....
....
....
....
....
....
....
....
....
....
....
....
....
....
....

....
....
....
....
....
....
....
....
....
....
....
....
....
....
....
....
....
....
....
....
....
....
....
....

....
....
....
....
....
....
....
....
....
....
....
....
....
....
....
....
....
....
....
....
....
....
....
....

WINTER

I wonder if the snow loves the
trees and fields, that it kisses
them so gently?

Lewis Carroll

INTRODUCTION

While you may think of winter as the bearer of a dormant world, there is still every reason to go outside and explore the countryside. Signs of activity can still be seen and heard, from the budding blossoms of the elder tree to the faint birdsong in the bare branches. If you still aren't persuaded by this, then the stunning sunrises and sunsets in the colder months are definitely worth getting out of bed for. Grab your scarf and gloves and experience the beauty of a country winter wonderland.

NATURE CALLS

Winter can seem quiet on the wildlife front with many animals bedding down, but there is still plenty to see. When you're out on a winter walk, listen out for the tawny owl and its familiar 'tu-whit tu-whoo' call, as winter is its courting season. Other sounds to listen out for are whooper swans honking, widgeons whistling, foxes barking and snipes screeching! Barn owls are forced out of hiding to hunt on clear days as their feathers aren't waterproof.

OWLS

There are five species of these beautiful nocturnal and crepuscular birds in the UK:

Barn owl – has a white heart-shaped face and buff-coloured wings and head.

Long-eared owl – has light brown feathers with dark brown streaks and orange eyes, with ear tufts (although they are not ears) that are raised when it feels under threat.

Short-eared owl – has mottled brown plumage with cream feathers on the underside of its wings, and yellow eyes.

Tawny owl – has reddish-brown feathers but with a ring of dark brown feathers framing its face.

Little owl – introduced into the UK in the nineteenth century, it has brown, cream and white plumage, and distinctive yellow eyes. This bird can often be seen hunting in daytime.

COUNTRY LORE

The grey heron has long been associated with bad news, especially for the Bishop of Chichester in West Sussex. An old saying goes that when the bishop is about to die, a heron will perch on the pinnacle of the cathedral spire.

ROBIN

The robin is a much-loved winter bird. Here are some facts you might not have known about this beautiful creature:

- The robin is related to the blackbird and the nightingale.

- Younger robins have brown breasts; it's only when they have their first moult that their plumage turns red.

- Robins eat anything from fruit to spiders, but their favourite meal is mealworms.

- The robin became Britain's national bird on 15 December 1960.

COUNTRY LORE

Robins are considered lucky. Wish upon the first robin you see in winter, and your wish will come true – but only if the robin remains in sight until you have finished saying your wish.

ANIMAL TRACKS

Aside from finding footprints and identifying them, there are other ways to determine animal activity, for example, if bark has been stripped off the trees it's likely that deer or squirrels are nearby and a pile of dove feathers could indicate that a bird of prey has eaten there recently; however, if the feathers have been bitten rather than plucked then it's more likely that a fox caught the unfortunate bird. Look out for the distinctive five-toed prints of the badger and for their setts, which often have large mounds of earth and tell-tale wiry hairs next to the entrance.

WEASELS

Common weasels can be sighted in Britain, Europe and the Mediterranean area but not the Mediterranean islands. They are similar in appearance to stoats but they don't have a black tip on the end of their tails. You can often find them in grasslands, forests and moors where they nest in holes or tree stumps. Weasels that live at high altitude and in the colder climes, such as the least weasel, the long-tailed weasel and the short-tailed weasel (otherwise known as a stoat), develop white coats in winter.

BRIMSTONE BUTTERFLY

Unlike other UK butterflies, this butterfly (that resembles two leaves) perches on evergreen branches throughout the winter months. Look carefully and you might be able to spot it covered in ice crystals as it waits for spring to thaw it.

QUEEN WASPS

Colonies of wasps, including hornets, die off in autumn, yet the queens survive the coldest months, when they are in search of a nesting place. You'll often see them flying around looking for places to live. It isn't uncommon that they will rest alongside other insects, such as earwigs and hoverflies, as if companions, until the warmer months arrive – when they become their prey.

COMMON FROG

The common frog can be spotted in the coldest of winters, swimming underneath the ice that has formed on top of rivers and lakes or hibernating under logs, due to its ability to slow down its metabolism and therefore survive the freezing temperatures.

THE SKY AT NIGHT

WATCH THE SUNSET

Spectacular sunsets can be enjoyed year-round but winter has some of the best. If the weather has been fine all day with clear skies and little cloud cover, make a special visit to the brow of a hill or local beauty spot to enjoy this stunning free light show.

Obviously the days are shorter in winter and it's cold, so pack a flask of something and head off at about three o'clock so you don't miss out!

Land really is the best art.

Andy Warhol

TIPS FOR PHOTOGRAPHING SUNSETS

1. Wait for the right clouds – stunning sunsets tend to occur on clear or partly cloudy days. Clouds that are patchy and wispy will create some interesting patterns. Flat, grey sheets of cloud will not light up as much.

2. Get there early – the best light usually occurs within a one-minute window, which happens roughly 15 minutes before or after the sunset. This means you need to get to your location at least half an hour before the sun sets, so that you can set up your shot.

3. Find the right place – getting to your location early also gives you time to find the perfect angle from which to take your photograph. Experiment with different compositions. Getting low to a body of water to capture the sunset's reflection can work well. Also look for interesting shapes or silhouettes which will add interest to the foreground, such as trees or people.

4. Choose where to place the horizon – a general rule of thumb is to place the horizon line in the bottom third of the photo when the sunset is brilliant, and in the top third of the photo if the sunset is a bit bland or if the most captivating part of the picture is a reflection on water or some silhouettes.

5. Protect your eyes – staring directly at the sun can damage your eyes. Try to frame your shot with the sun just out of eyesight and then reposition your camera to take your shot. If the sun is very low in the sky and is diffused by cloud or haze, this shouldn't be as much of a problem.

6. Hang around after the sun has set – remember: the best lighting often happens after a sunset, so hang around for 15–30 minutes after the sun has disappeared below the horizon and you might be rewarded with some spectacular colours.

If you're in the country, take nothing but pictures, leave nothing but footprints, kill nothing but time.

Hunter Davies

MOONLIT WALKS

Don't let the cold weather put you off going for a walk! Here are some tips to keep you safe and warm when you head outside:

- The days are shorter in winter so plan your walks carefully – head out early to make the most the daylight and take short routes if you are setting off later in the day (take a torch just in case).

- Regardless of how much sunlight there is, take water with you. Dry winter air is dehydrating and you will also lose water through sweat.

- Wear several layers. Temperatures can be very changeable and it's best to be able to take layers on and off as required. Steer clear of cotton and wear clothes which are designed to wick moisture away from your skin, so you don't get cold.

- Don't forget your hat – around 20 to 60 per cent of heat is lost through an uncovered head. A scarf and gloves are a good idea, particularly if you are walking in the hills or near the windy coast, and natural wool socks will keep your feet nice and cosy.

FANCY A TIPPLE?

If you're embarking on a winter walk, you might consider taking a tippling cane with you. It's a type of walking stick with a small flask concealed inside, making it ideal for taking a discreet dram on a cold day, although it has been documented that alcohol doesn't actually warm you in its truest sense, so best take a flask of tea with you too!

In every walk with nature one receives far more than he seeks.

John Muir, from *Steep Trails*

STARGAZING LOCATIONS

The UK has some of the largest areas of dark sky in Europe, which means it's a great place to view stars at night. The best areas to stargaze are away from light pollution. For this reason, many of our forests and parks are perfect stargazing spots, including Galloway Forest Park in Scotland, Exmoor, Northumberland and South Downs National Parks in England, and Elan Valley in Wales. The Brecon Beacons and Snowdonia both carry Dark Sky Reserve status.

Other internationally recognised 'Dark Sky Places' include Mont-Mégantic in Quebec, Canada; Aoraki Mackenzie in New Zealand; the NamibRand Nature Reserve in southern Namibia; and Westhavelland (Germany).

GUIDANCE FROM ABOVE

If out walking at night, you can find north simply by reading the stars. Look for the group of seven stars known as the 'Plough' or 'Big Dipper', which resembles a saucepan. Identify the 'pointer' stars – the ones that soup would run off if you tipped the saucepan. The North Star is above these two pointer stars and true north lies directly underneath the North Star.

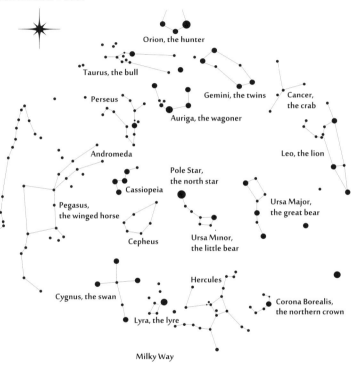

NORTHERN SKY

Orion, the hunter

Taurus, the bull

Perseus

Gemini, the twins

Cancer, the crab

Auriga, the wagoner

Andromeda

Leo, the lion

Pole Star, the north star

Cassiopeia

Pegasus, the winged horse

Ursa Major, the great bear

Cepheus

Ursa Minor, the little bear

Hercules

Cygnus, the swan

Corona Borealis, the northern crown

Lyra, the lyre

Milky Way

SOUTHERN SKY

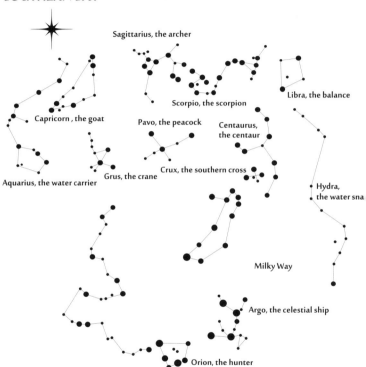

Sagittarius, the archer

Capricorn , the goat

Scorpio, the scorpion

Libra, the balance

Pavo, the peacock

Centaurus,
the centaur

Aquarius, the water carrier

Grus, the crane

Crux, the southern cross

Hydra,
the water sna

Milky Way

Argo, the celestial ship

Orion, the hunter

WINTER WALKS

STEADY AS YOU GO!

When the ground is frozen it can make walking treacherous. One way to ensure that you don't slip up and hurt yourself is to invest in a set of walking poles or a stick. The traditional walking stick is made of ash, not only for its strength but because it is believed to possess magical properties. It is also believed to be the best type of walking stick for killing snakes swiftly! Emigrants travelling by ship from Ireland to the United States in the nineteenth century carried twigs from a descendant of the sacred ash, the Tree of Creevna, to protect themselves from drowning.

STAYING SNUG

Whether you're on a winter walk or messing about in the snow, layering your clothes will help you keep warm without overheating. A base layer should be the first thing you put on – aim for something that fits snugly against your body; a long-sleeved merino wool top is a great option. Next, put on your middle layer, which should be light and fit loosely; a fleece will work well for this. Your outer layer should be something like a windproof, waterproof jacket with a hood. As you're using layers, you will be free to remove an item of clothing if you feel you're getting too warm and replace the layer if you need to!

CHALK FIGURES

Chalk-hill figures are some of the most striking features of southern England's downlands. Some of these huge depictions of man and beast, created by cutting away the turf and soil to reveal the chalk beneath, are believed to date back to the Celts in 500 BC as a celebration of the gods that they worshipped. Some examples include:

- **Long Man of Wilmington, Windover Hill, East Sussex**

- **Cerne Abbas Giant, Dorchester, Dorset**

- **Uffington White Horse, Oxfordshire**

Giant 'land pictures' and artworks (or geoglyphs) are also found in Peru, Chile, Brazil, California, Australia and Russia.

NATURAL NAVIGATOR

Moss can help with navigation. Look for a vertical surface where moss is growing – if at half a metre up on the surface moss is present, it is likely to be on the north side, as this is the side in shade during the full heat of the day and therefore it remains moist, allowing moss to thrive.

Earth and sky, woods
and fields, lakes and
rivers, the mountain
and the sea, are excellent
schoolmasters.

John Lubbock, from *The Use of Life*

Nature is the art of God.

Dante Alighieri

TALLEST PEAKS IN THE UK AND EUROPE

- Mount Elbrus, Russia: 5,642 m
- Mount Shkhara, Georgia: 5,193 m
- Mount Blanc, France/Italy: 4,808 m
- Mount Rosa, Switzerland: 4,634 m
- Mount Bazardüzü, Azerbaijan: 4,466 m
- Ben Nevis, Scotland: 1,344 m
- Snowdon, Wales: 1,085 m
- Scafell Pike, England: 978 m
- Slieve Donard, Northern Ireland: 850 m

Great things are done when
Men & Mountains meet
This is not Done by
Jostling in the Street

William Blake

FORAGING FUN

WHITTLE ME THIS

Picking up kindling for wood fires once the nights draw in can be a fun way to pass the time on a woodland walk, but there is something else that you can use these short lengths of wood for and that's whittling! This is the art of carving shapes from wood with a pocketknife – simple items to make include a boat, a slingshot and tools.

HOW TO CARVE A MUG

Equipment
A dry, solid log which is about the thickness of a large mug
Knife
Water
Sandpaper
Embers from a fire
Mineral oil

Method

1. Find a suitable log (ideally oak or ash).

2. Remove the outer bark with your knife and carve in a small hole in the top of the log.

3. Take an ember from your fire and place it in the hole, blowing gently on it to set it alight.

4. Add more embers as they burn out the mug (every now and then you'll need to scrape out the mug and apply new embers).

5. Once you're happy with the shape of your mug, scrape off the charcoal and plunge it into water to put the ember out.

6. Sand down the inside of the mug, then clean it and apply a little mineral oil to seal it.

MISTLETOE AND VINE

Look out for cheerful bundles of mistletoe nestled in the branches of trees and shrubs. Despite its association with romance and good cheer, the mistletoe plant is actually parasitic and uses the trees it grows in as a host. Its seeds are spread by the droppings of birds which feed on its berries, such as the mistlethrush, which is often why the plant is found high up in a tree. When used as a Christmas decoration, custom dictates that the mistletoe must not touch the ground between its cutting and its removal as the last of the Christmas greens at Candlemas.

Nature's peace will flow
into you as sunshine
flows into trees.

John Muir

MAKING A WREATH

Why buy a wreath when you can make one out of the materials you have foraged on your walk?

Equipment

Two wire coat hangers
Branches of greenery, such as redwood, pine, Douglas or fir
Florist tape
Floral wire
Hot glue
Decorations, such as ribbon and pine cones

Method

1. Bend the coat hangers to make two circles, keeping the hooks in their original shape. Put one on top of the other and secure with floral tape.

2. Cut the branches that you have collected to around eight inches long. Fix each branch to the

base of the wreath with floral wire overlapping the stems so that the wire is hidden.

3. Add your decorations to the wreath and use hot glue or floral wire to secure.

4. To spice up the decorations, add glitter to the pine cones. Clean the cone with boiling water and leave to dry, then paint glue onto its tips with a brush and sprinkle glitter onto the glue. If you want to make the ribbon look more interesting, cut it into smaller lengths and tie them into mini bows.

Today I have grown taller from walking with the trees.

Karle Wilson Baker

THERAPY VIA NATURE

TREE HUGGING

Hugging a tree may sound like a thing hippies do but there is growing evidence that trees are good for our mental health. Studies show trees can improve depression, Attention Deficit Hyperactivity Disorder (ADHD), headaches, stress and concentration levels. Why do trees have such a powerful effect on us? It's thought that we have an innate need to live among plants and trees, just as our ancestors did. In addition, research suggests that trees release phytoncides (wood essential oils), which reduce our blood pressure and improve mood, sleep and energy levels.

You don't have to touch a tree to receive its benefits. Just being near trees can make you healthier. In Japan, people practise 'forest bathing', taking long walks through ancient forests in order to rejuvenate their minds and bodies, and boost their immune systems. So spend some time sitting beneath your favourite tree. (You can work your way up to giving it a cuddle.)

NOTES

....
....
....
....
....
....
....
....
....
....
....
....
....
....
....
....
....
....
....

....
....
....
....
....
....
....
....
....
....
....
....
....
....
....
....
....
....
....
....
....
....
....

....
....
....
....
....
....
....
....
....
....
....
....
....
....
....
....
....
....
....
....
....
....
....

COUNTRY WISDOM

There is nothing quite like experiencing the natural world by getting out into the fresh air, so do your part to preserve this special privilege and always be mindful when wandering through the countryside. If you'd like to get involved further in keeping your local countryside green and pleasant, why not enquire at your local council about volunteering at a wildlife trust nearby? For volunteering on a grander scale, check out www.nationaltrust.org.uk/get-involved/volunteer to see how you can help one of the UK's foremost conservation charities continue in their valuable work.

At some point in life,
the world's beauty
becomes enough.

Toni Morrison

FURTHER READING

BIRDS

Barnes, Simon *Birdwatching with Your Eyes Closed: An Introduction to Birdsong* (2012, Short Books)

Bewick, Thomas *Bewick's British Birds* (2010, Arcturus)

Elphick, Jonathan; Svensson, Lars; Pedersen, Jan *Birdsong: 150 British and Irish Birds and Their Amazing Sounds* (2012, Quadrille)

Holden, Peter; Cleves, Tim *RSPB Handbook of British Birds* (2010, Christopher Helm)

COUNTRY LORE

Binney, Ruth *The English Countryside: Amazing and Extraordinary Facts* (2011, David and Charles)

Carr-Gomm, Phillip; Heygate, Richard *The Book of English Magic* (2010, John Murray)

Peyton, Jane *Brilliant Britain* (2012, Summersdale)

Rhodes, Chloe *One for Sorrow: A Book of Old-fashioned Lore* (2011, Michael O'Mara)

Struthers, Jane *Red Sky at Night: The Book of Lost Country Wisdom* (2009, Ebury)

FLOWERS

Fletcher, Neil *Wild Flowers* (2010, Dorling Kindersley)

Mabey, Richard *Flora Britannica* (1996, Chatto & Windus)

Sutton, David *Green Guide to Wild Flowers of Britain and Europe* (2001, New Holland)

FORAGING WILD FOOD

Eastoe, Jane *Wild Food: Foraging for Food in the Wild* (2008, Anova)

Irving, Miles *The Forager Handbook* (2009, Ebury)

Mabey, Richard *Food for Free* (2012, Collins)

WALKS

Bathurst, David *Walking the South Coast of England* (2008, Summersdale)

Gooley, Tristan *The Natural Navigator* (2010, Virgin Books)

Palmer, Jude *The Walker's Friend* (2010, Summersdale)

Thompson, Elspeth *The Wonderful Weekend Book* (2010, John Murray)

Williamson, Richard *52 West Sussex Walks* (2012, Summersdale)

WEATHER

Hamblyn, Richard *The Cloud Book: How to Understand the Skies* (2008, David and Charles)

The MET Office Book of the British Weather: UK Weather Month by Month (2010, David and Charles)

Pretor-Pinney, Gavin *The Cloud Collector's Handbook* (2009, Sceptre)

ONLINE RESOURCES

www.nationaltrust.org.uk
www.princescountrysidefund.org.uk
www.ramblers.org.uk
www.wcl.org.uk
www.woodlandtrust.org.uk

If you're interested in finding out more
about our books, find us on Facebook at
Summersdale Publishers and follow us on
Twitter at **@Summersdale**.

www.summersdale.com